You Know You're Over 50 When...

by Herbert I. Kavet
Illustrated by Martin Riskin
Layout by CoffeyCup Productions

©1997 by Boston America Corp.

30 29 28 27 26 25 24 23 22 21 20 19 18 17 16 15 14 13 12 11 10 9 8 7 6 5 4

W9-CHX-397

Boston America Corp.
125 Walnut Street, Watertown, MA 02172   617-923-1111 Fax: 617-923-8839

INTRODUCTION

In the olden days hardly anyone reached the age of 50. The reasons for this are unknown and are still being studied by archeologists. But, in modern times, many young fellows reach their 50th birthday while feeling and sometimes looking much younger. Since few brave souls can picture themselves "HALF A CENTURY" old, this book will give people suspicious of nearing this mark a few tips on how to identify themselves.

You Know You're Over 50 When...

You add "GOD WILLING" to end of
most of your statements.

You Know You're Over 50 When...

You are absolutely positive they build stairs steeper these days.

You Know You're Over 50 When...

Someone calls you "POPS." (Sometimes someone calls you "CHIEF" or even a seemingly middle-aged gent calls you "SIR" or "MISTER.")

You Know You're Over 50 When...

You keep forgetting. No matter how many diaries, appointment books, or calenders you have, you still forget. You write notes on slips of paper and then forget where you put the slips of paper and then forget where you put the slips. Sometimes you call your kids by the wrong names.

You Know You're Over 50 When...

All the money you saved for years
for your children's college education
just about covers the first semester.

You Know You're Over 50 When...

Your arms aren't long enough to hold
your reading material.

You Know You're Over 50 When...

You remember when "Made in Japan" meant something didn't work.

You Know You're Over 50 When...

You don't care where your wife goes when she goes out, as long as you don't have to go with her.

You Know You're Over 50 When...

Getting a little action means
your prune juice is working.

You Know You're Over 50 When...

You start believing the ads for hemmorrhoid, constipation, and hair loss remedies.

You Know You're Over 50 When...

You still think of "grass" as something you cut. You remember when smoking cigarettes was fashionable.

You Know You're Over 50 When...

Attractive women at the office feel
safe enough to flirt outrageously with you.

You Know You're Over 50 When...

You start to hang around with new grandparents. Of course, most of them are much older than you are.

You Know You're Over 50 When...

Watching sports on T.V. seems to be a much more sensible pastime than risking tearing yourself apart by playing the sports yourself.

You Know You're Over 50 When...

Your music isn't their music.

You Know You're Over 50 When...

Your kids are making more money than you.
("Johnny's daddy" has been changed to
"the Doctor's father".)

You Know You're Over 50 When...

No matter how many push-ups and sit-ups you do, and no matter how far you run, finally resign yourself to no longer being a "HUNK."

You Know You're Over 50 When...

You feel like the "morning after" and you can swear you haven't been anywhere.

You Know You're Over 50 When...

You sit down to put on your underwear. The young guys in the locker rooms have colored shorts but yours are all white.

You Know You're Over 50 When...

You give up trying to learn the names of all those African countries. At least you could spell the Belgian Congo and Rhodesia.

You Know You're Over 50 When...

Picking up the balls seems to be almost
as much work as it used to be playing the game.

You Know You're Over 50 When...

You choose your cars for comfort and productivity rather than sex appeal, unless you are single again in which case you opt for total outrageousness.

You Know You're Over 50 When...

Instead of combing your hair you start arranging it. There is more hair on your chest than on your head.

You Know You're Over 50 When...

The sports you do participate in require the use of braces, bandages, and protective gear that draw pitying glances from spectators.

You Know You're Over 50 When...

Your back hurts. You see doctors, osteopaths, chiropractors, and therapists; you change your mattress, buy special shoes, wear braces, do exercises, take pills, and hang upside down, and it still hurts.

You Know You're Over 50 When...

People keep saying "You haven't changed."
This is the culmination of the 3 stages of life;
youth, middle age, and YOU HAVEN'T CHANGED.

You Know You're Over 50 When...

People you used to hold in awe like doctors, policemen, and clergymen start being younger than you.

You Know You're Over 50 When...

You start dressing for comfort rather than blindly following the latest fashions. Your color coordination takes a back seat to expediency.

You Know You're Over 50 When...

You are finally smart enough to
hire a kid to mow your lawn.

You Know You're Over 50 When...

You may still be in the "rat race"
but you no longer feel you have to win it.

You Know You're Over 50 When...

You don't always wake up "aroused"
like you used to every day.

You Know You're Over 50 When...

You eat less and less and yet
you still continue to gain weight.

You Know You're Over 50 When...

You are vaguely suspicious of "new" food such as sprouts, tofu, sushi, and seeds.

You Know You're Over 50 When...

Your kid's motorbike costs more than
your 1949 DeSoto did.

You Know You're Over 50 When...

You have hats in your clost but never wear them anymore. You don't throw them out because you can never know when they might come back in style.

You Know You're Over 50 When...

Growing melons brings you almost as much satisfaction as fondling them once did. You remember when "boobs" referred to dumb kids.

You Know You're Over 50 When...

55 MPH seems a very reasonable and
safe speed to travel at.

You Know You're Over 50 When...

All the things you threw out the last time you moved now seem to be "Collectors item"s and worth a fortune.

You Know You're Over 50 When...

You really have to concentrate to call "Girls" "Women". You remember when calling "Women "Girls" was a compliment. Your not quite sure if you're allowed to call them "Ladies."

You Know You're Over 50 When...

You see your old cereal bowl
in an antique shop.

You Know You're Over 50 When...

You meet old friends and you tell each other
"YOU HAVEN'T CHANGED A BIT."

You Know You're Over 50 When...

Your name appears on every mail order list in the country.

You Know You're Over 50 When...

You still feel your youthful ardor,
but only once in a while.

You Know You're Over 50 When...

You have a very special comfortable chair
from which it is very difficult to remove you.

You Know You're Over 50 When...

You recognize that middle age spread
only serves to bring people closer together.

You Know You're Over 50 When...

You're smart enough not to take out
all the garbage in one trip.

You Know You're Over 50 When...

You no longer brag about
how many parking ticketsyou have.

You Know You're Over 50 When...

You never owned edible underwear.

You Know You're Over 50 When...

You remember to stop the newspapers
before going on vacation.

You Know You're Over 50 When...

Everybody has already heard
all your jokes.

You Know You're Over 50 When...

You never run out of toilet paper.

You Know You're Over 50 When...

You feel most comfortable straddling two lanes.

You Know You're Over 50 When...

You don't go to nude beaches.

You Know You're Over 50 When...

You pay your phone and electric bills
before they are due.

You Know You're Over 50 When...

No one cares anymore
what you did in high school.

You Know You're Over 50 When...

You find yourself squinting during candle light dinners.

You Know You're Over 50 When...

You are resigned to the fact
that certain foods just aren't compatible
with your gastrointestinal system.

You Know You're Over 50 When...

You start to look forward
to dull evenings at home.

You Know You're Over 50 When...

Pretty much everything you own is paid for.
You can finally afford lots of things
that you no longer want.

You Know You're Over 50 When...

You no longer bounce checks.

You Know You're Over 50 When...

Your stomach gets upset if you eat raw cookie dough.

OTHER GREAT BOOKS BY BOSTON AMERICA

The fine, cultivated stores carrying our books really get ticked if you buy directly from the publisher so if you can, please patronize your local store and let them make a buck. If, however, the fools don't carry a particular title, you can order them from us for $7, postpaid. Credit cards accepted for orders of 4 or more books.

#2400 How To Have Sex On Your Birthday
Finding a partner, special birthday sex positions, kinky sex and much more

#2403 The Good Bonking Guide
Bonking is a very useful British term for "you know what" and this book covers bonking in the dark, bonking all night long, improving your bonking and everything else you might want to know.

#2419 Cucumbers Are Better Than Men Because...
Cucumbers never go soft in a second, aren't afraid of commitment and never criticize.

#2423 Is There Sex After 40
It says normal couples do it at least once a week, you get the urge but can't remember what for and "if he was rigid I wouldn't be frigid".

#2424 Is There Sex After 50
Swapping him for two 25 year olds, being into gardening, wine making and group sex and liking it better when the bulge was in his trousers.

#2430 Is There Sex After 30
Being too tired to get it up, thinking kinky is leaving the lights on and remembering when you could do it 3 times a night.

#2432 Big Weenies
Big weenies and small weenies and all their names and how to find big weenies in a strange town and how to rate them.

#2434 Sex and Marriage
Wives wanting foreplay and romance and husbands wanting to be allowed to go to sleep right after. Techniques for improving your wife or husband or ignoring them.

#2438 Dog Farts
Dogs get blames for lots of farts they don't do but this book gives all the real ones like the sleeping dog fart and the living room fart.

#2446 The PMS Book
This book covers all the problems from irritability to clumsiness to chocolate craving to backaches in a funny and sympathetic manner.

#2450 How To Pick Up Girls
This book holds the keys to understanding women and teaches never fail lines plus places to meet shy, drunk weird and even naked girls

#2451 How To Pick Up Guys
How to get them to grovel at your feet and how to spot the losers and how to get rid of them after sex.

#2453 Beginners Sex Manual
Covers basics such as how to tell if you're a virgin and good things to say before and after sex.

#2455 Unspeakably Rotten Cartoons
Words cannot describe this totally tasteless and crass collection of cartoons that are guaranteed to offend and make you laugh.

#2457 Hooters
This is a photo book of the latest lingo for boobs and bosoms and bulging breasts.

#2458 Adult Connect The Dots
If you can count and use a pencil at the same time you too can be a pornographer.

#2463 Butts and Buns
These photos take a racy, rear view at women's tushes, beautiful buns and delicate derrieres.

#2465 Do It Yourself Guide To Safe Sex
Well if you do it yourself you can get it right the first time and never catch any nasty diseases.

#2466 Guide To Intimate Apparel
Photos and purposes of all the lacy lingerie and unmentionables from bloomers to garters to wedgies.

#2469 Hunks
A list of all the popular men's names and how they compare in bed and boardroom and physical sizes,

#2470 How To Find A Man And Get Married In 30 Days
Reserve the hall first and then learn ways and places to meet men, how to use sex and how to get rid of your mistakes,

#2471 Student Guide To Farting
The roommate fart, the math teacher fart, the lunch lady fart. This book covers them all.

#2472 Party Games For 30 Year Olds
New racy games and lists of old favorites. This book has them all and will keep a party of 30 year olds going all night.

#2473 Party Games For 40 Year Olds
Similar to the 30 year old book with perhaps more emphasis on sex rather than drinking.

#2474 Party Games For 50 Year Olds
Just like the 30 and 40 year old games but this book gives instruction on keeping the players awake after 10 PM

#2501 Cowards Guide To Body Piercing
Cartoons and explanations of all the good and horrible places you can put holes in yourself.

#2502 Toilet Tips
Urinal etiquette and handling warm toilet seats or doors with lousy locks or smells that are not your own. A must for anyone that uses toilets.

#2503 Kinky World Records
Like the world's hairiest armpits or thickest condom or shortest male organ or longest time to take off a bra. Hey, you could set your own records.

#2504 Pregnant Woman's Guide To Farting
The Claustrophobia Fart and the Waiting Room Fart and the Naming the Baby Fart and the Constipation Fart are just a few.

#2505 Is There Sex After Retirement
Cartoons for the retired set such as, "If he was rigid I wouldn't b frigid" and "Of course I'll respect you in the morning you blind old bat. I'm your husband.

#2506 Farting Under The Covers And Other Secrets Of Successful Marriage.
Secret things husbands and wives do, secrets of regularity and secrets of listening to your wife.

#2700 Rules For Sex On Your Wedding Night
Rules for sex on the way to the hotel and rules for keeping up your energy and rules for couples who have been living together for 2 years.

#2701 Dictionary Of Doodie
Feels Like Shit, Shit Head, Shit On A Shingle, Shit Talk and all the other colorful uses of this most important word in the English language.

#2702 Alien Doodle Book
Doodle in all your favorite Aliens in ridiculous sexual escapades with humans.

#2703 You Know Your A Golf Addict When....
When you hustle your grandma, watch golf videos and think you look attractive in golf clothes.

#2704 What Every Woman Can Learn From Her Cat
An unmade bed is fluffier, there's no problem that can't be helped by a nap and when you want a little attention, roll over on your back.

#2705 Adult Connect The Dots
If you can count from 1 to 100 you can be a pornographer. You won't believe the results of your creativity

#1100 The 3 Stooges Book Of Party Games
You want to have a good party? Soitenly. So grab a few games from this riotous book.

BOSTON AMERICA C★O★R★P

125 Walnut Street, Watertown, MA 02172   (617) 923-1111   FAX: (617) 923-8839